I Am Mars

REBECCA AND JAMES MCDONALD

I Am Mars

Copyright © 2019 by Rebecca and James McDonald

All rights reserved. No part of this publication may be reproduced, stored, or distributed in any form or by any means, electronic or mechanical, including photocopy, recording, or any information storage and retrieval system, without prior permission in writing from the publisher and copyright owner.

ISBN: 978-0-9982949-8-8
First House of Lore paperback edition, 2019
Visit us at www.HouseOfLore.net

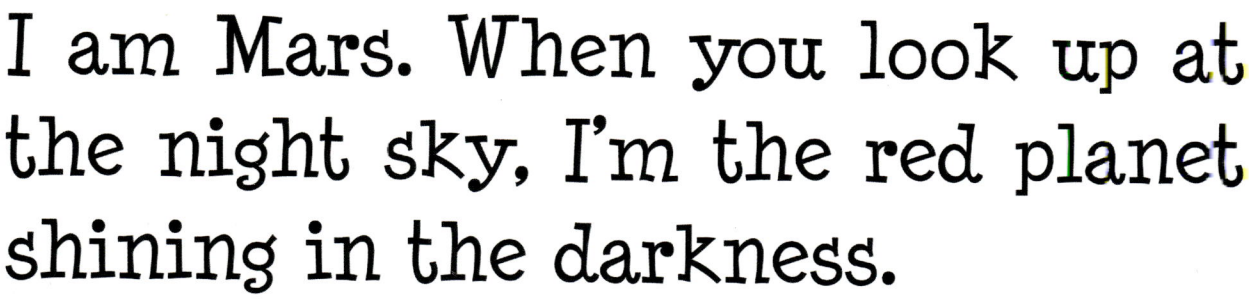

I am Mars. When you look up at the night sky, I'm the red planet shining in the darkness.

There are eight planets in our solar system that orbit the Sun. I'm the fourth planet away from the Sun, so it gets really cold on my surface.

Out of all the other planets in our solar system, it's me, Mars, that has the tallest mountain! Scientists call it Olympus Mons. It's three times taller than the tallest mountain on Earth.

When a spacecraft lands on my surface and stays in one place, it's called a lander. There are even robotic vehicles that roam around my surface. They're called rovers.

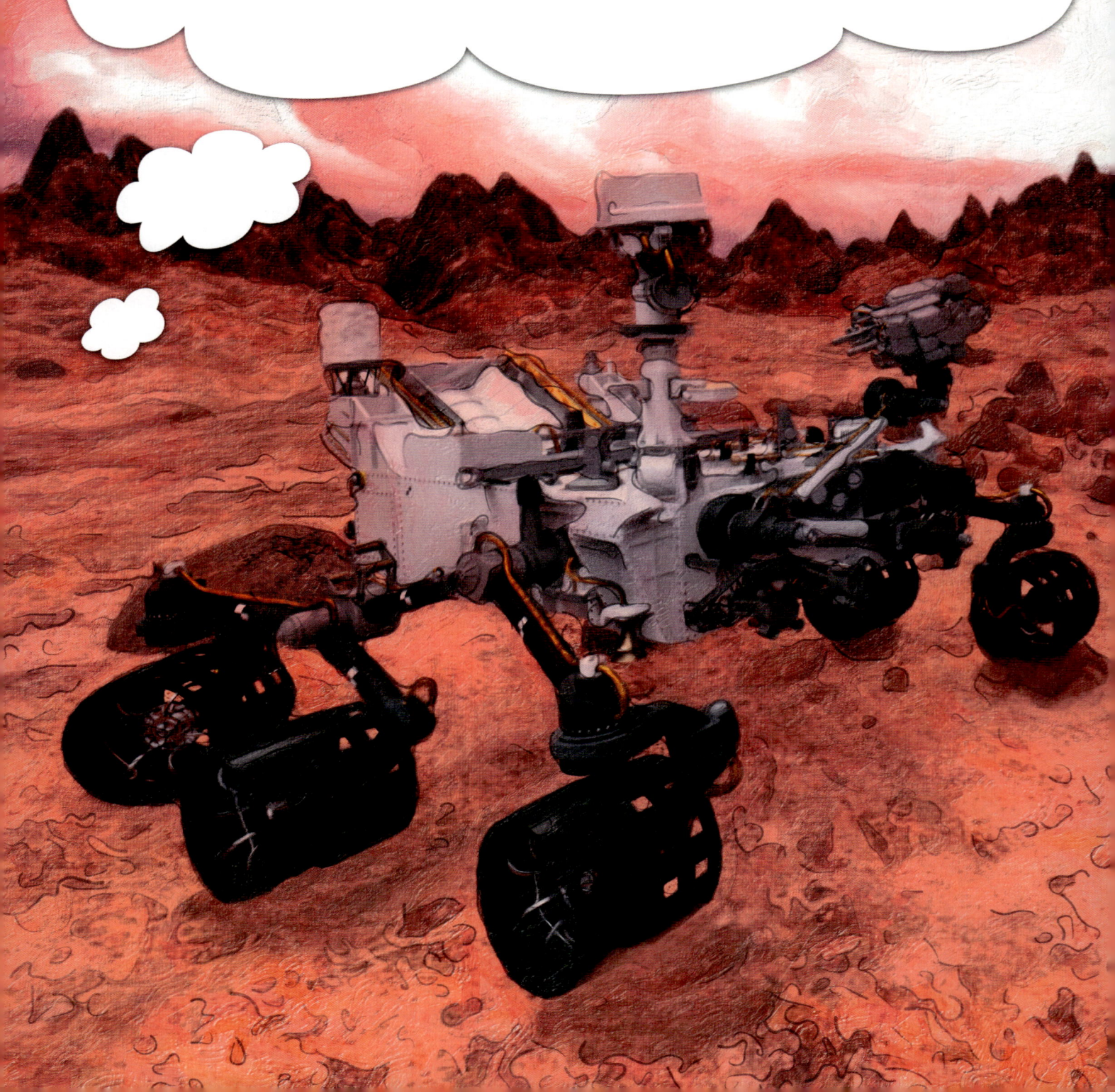

Out of all the spacecraft that have been watching from above and the rovers traveling over my surface, not one of them has ever seen any signs that there is life on me. There aren't any plants, animals or people.

Scientists have seen signs of water on my surface, but for people making the long journey to visit me, they will have to make sure to have enough water for the entire trip.

What do you think people traveling to Mars will need to bring?

What do you think a spacesuit will look like for exploring Mars?

Can you draw a picture of what you think a spaceship will look like that can travel to Mars?

Can you draw a space station?

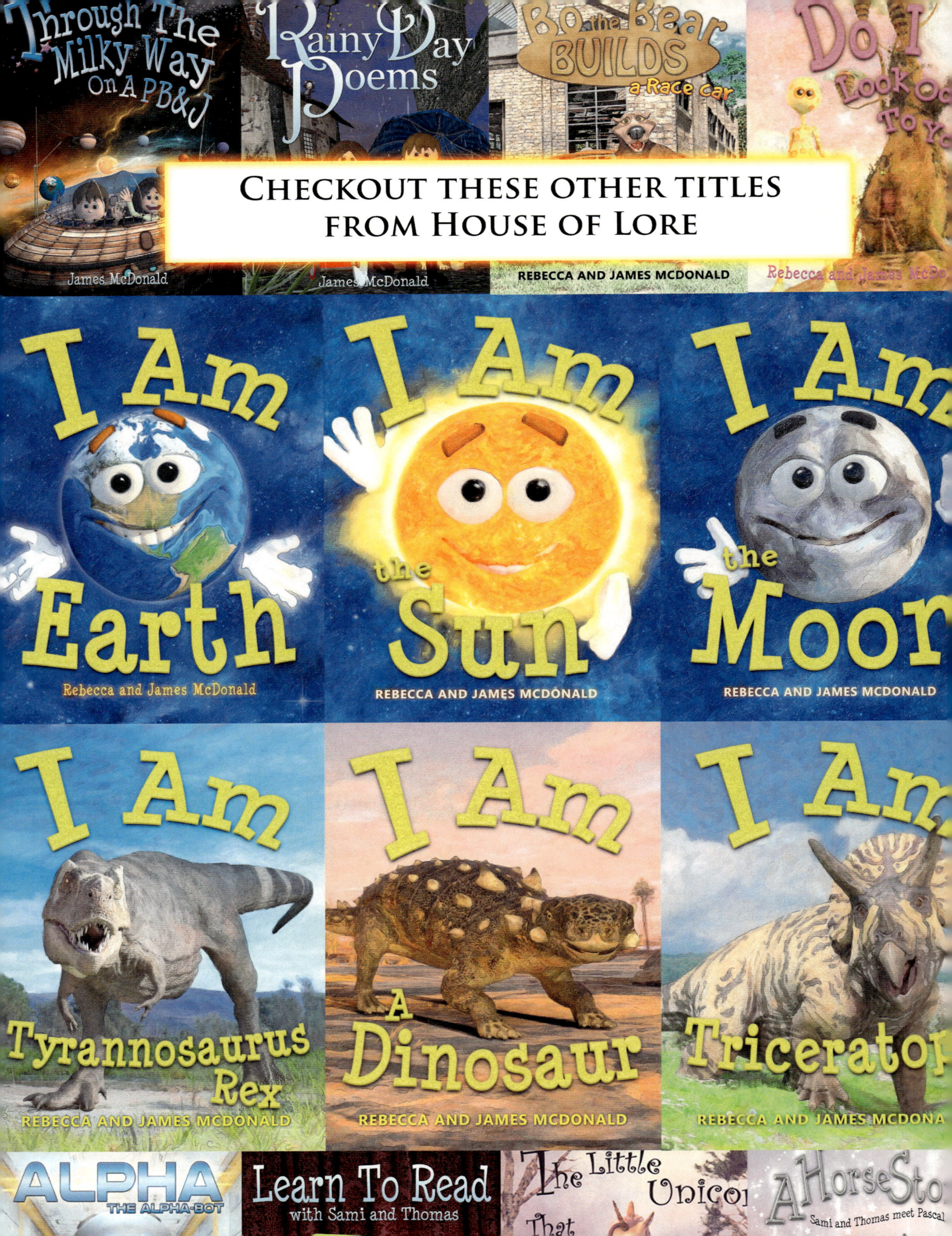

Made in the USA
Monee, IL
11 June 2021